l knowing. b...

Buddha, excep...

n. For those of quiet taste, he...

you a bit apart, contemplati...

as if beneath all feeling wer...

ns his back and sits motionle...

at comes or goes behind him.

unforgettable. He faces you

M000279101

FOR

_____

FROM

_____

DATE

_____

Poems for Cat Lovers

WATERCOLORS BY
JO ANNA POEHLMANN

IDEALS PUBLICATIONS
NASHVILLE, TENNESSEE

ISBN 0-8249-5851-9

Published by Ideals Publications
A division of Guideposts
535 Metroplex Drive, Suite 250
Nashville, Tennessee 37211
www.idealsbooks.com

Copyright © 2003 by Ideals Publications

All rights reserved. No part of this publication may be reproduced or transmitted in any
form or by any means, electronic or mechanical, including photocopy, recording, or any
information storage and retrieval system, without permission in writing from the publisher.

Color separations by Precision Color Graphics, Franklin, Wisconsin
Caseside printed in the U.S.A.
Text printed and bound in Mexico by RR Donnelley

Library of Congress CIP data on file

10 9 8 7 6 5 4 3 2 1

POEMS SELECTED BY LISA C. RAGAN
SERIES DESIGN BY EVE DEGRIE
BOOK DESIGN BY JENNY EBER HANCOCK

ACKNOWLEDGMENTS

BENÉT, WILLIAM ROSE. "The Little Cats" from *The Stairway of Surprise*. Copyright © 1947 by the author. Used by permission of
James Benét. BURDEN, JEAN. "For a Yellow Cat at Midnight." Originally appeared in *The Southern Review*, May 29, 1971, Louisiana
State University Press, and subsequently in *A Celebration of Cats* compiled by Jean Burden. Published by Paul S. Eriksson, Inc., NY
and in *Taking Light from Each Other, University Press of Florida*, 1992. Used by permission of Jean Burden. COATSWORTH, ELIZABETH.
"The Open Door" from *Away Goes Sally* by Elizabeth Coatsworth. Copyright © 1934 by Macmillan Publishing Company and
renewed in 1962 by Elizabeth Coatsworth Beston. "Portrait of a Young Cat" and "On a Night of Snow" from *Night and the Cat*.
Copyright © 1950 and published by the Macmillan Company. Used by permission of Patterson Marsh Ltd. FARJEON, ELEANOR.
"Cats" from *The Children's Bells*. Copyright © 1960 by Eleanor Farjeon. Published by Henry C. Walck, Inc. Used by permission of
Harold Ober Associates, Inc. HARRIMAN, DOROTHY. "Cat on a Porch at Dusk" from *The Christian Science Monitor*. Reproduced with
permission. Copyright © 1952 by *The Christian Science Monitor*. HAYES, EVELYN. "A Garden Lion." from *A Garden in the Antipodes*.
Copyright © 1929 by the author. Used courtesy of Macmillan Publishers, Ltd., London. KIRKUP, JAMES. "To Puffin, a White Cat"
from *A Correct Compassion and Other Poems*. Copyright © 1952 by the author. "The Bird Fancier" from *Refusal to Conform*. Copyright © 1963 by the author. Poems used by permission of James Kirkup. KUSKIN, KARLA. "This Cat" from *Near the Window Tree*.

(continued on p. 88)

CONTENTS

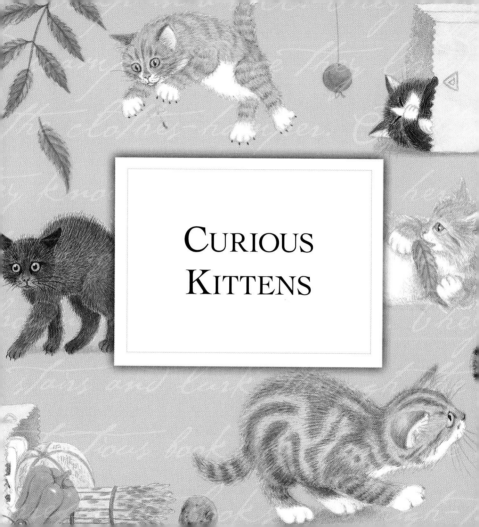

CURIOUS
KITTENS

In the Image of the Lion

Wild beasts he created later,
Lions with their paws so furious;
In the image of the lion
Made he kittens small and curious.

— HEINRICH HEINE
TRANSLATED BY E. A. BOWRING

MOTHER CAT'S PURR

Sleep the half-sleep,
Kittens dear,
While your mother
Catnaps near.

Every kitten
Is a cat,
And you must
Remember that

POEMS FOR CAT LOVERS

Naps for cats
Are mostly fake;
Any time
Is time to wake,

Or time to pounce,
Or time to scat.
That's what sleep is—
For a cat.
—JANE YOLEN

KITTEN

The black kitten,
Arched stiff,
Dances sidewise
From behind
The chair, leaps,
Tears away with
Ears back, spins,
Lands crouched
Flat on the floor;
Sighting something
At nose level—

Her eyes round
As oranges, her
Hind legs marking
Time—then she
Pounces, cactus-clawed
Upon a strayed
Strand of fluff.
Can anyone
Believe that she
Doesn't ask us
To laugh?
—VALERIE WORTH

from THE KITTEN AND FALLING LEAVES

See the kitten on the wall,
Sporting with the leaves that fall,
Withered leaves—one, two, and three—
From the lofty elder tree! . . .
With a tiger leap halfway
Now she meets the coming prey,
Lets it go as fast, and then
Has it in her power again.
Now she works with three or four,
Like an Indian conjurer;
Quick as he in feats of art,
Far beyond in joy of heart.

—WILLIAM WORDSWORTH

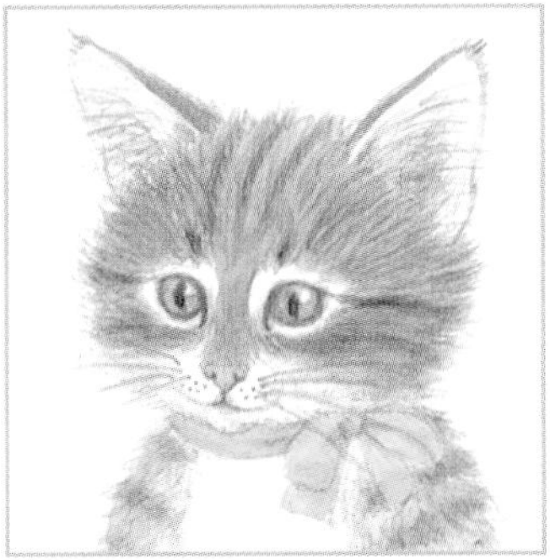

THE LITTLE CATS

Our mackerel cat
Has three kittens.
The girl one sat
With white mittens
Down in the hall.
The grandfather clock
Bonged. The kitten
Shied at the shock.

Pounce, bounce,
Come her two brothers.
There were once
Three others.
We don't surmise
Who their sire is.
Their round eyes
Are all iris.

They sleep in a ball.
They scuffle and scamper.
Once they lived all
By the clothes-hamper.
Of their mother they know
They can't boss her.
They sit in a row
For the milk saucer.

They think a brown marble
Is a mouse.
They hop up stairs
And lurk through the house.
Pretentious books
By many are written.
I prefer the looks
Of a high-tail kitten.

—WILLIAM ROSE BENÉT

CURIOUS KITTENS   15

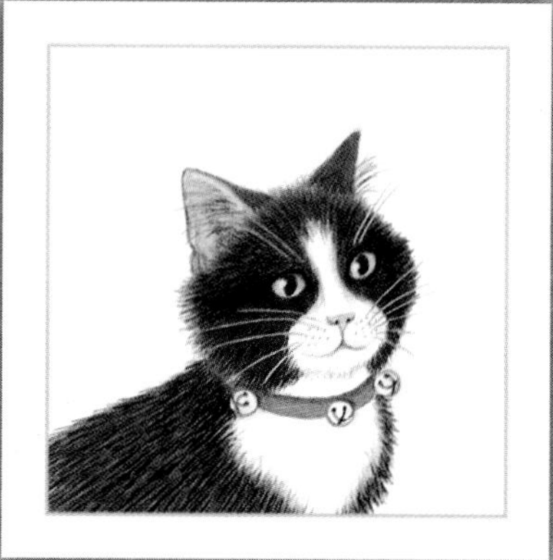

Miss Tibbles

Miss Tibbles is my kitten; white
as day she is and black as night.
She moves in little gusts and breezes
sharp and sudden as a sneeze is.

At hunting Tibbles has no match.
How I like to see her catch
moth or beetle, two-a-penny,
and feast until there isn't any!

Sometimes I like her calm, unwild,
gentle as a sleeping child,
and wonder as she lies, a fur ring
curled upon my lap, unstirring,
is it me or Tibbles purring?

—Ian Serraillier

THE KITTEN

Always it's pouncing at nothing,
Striking with both paws at once.
Although there is nothing to see,
It seems the kitten sees something,
Or that he's compelled to exert
Such force as he is supplied with—
Must exert it, practice it—
Even on nothing at all.

The attraction of nothing at all?
Imagination, maybe—
Present even in kittens—
Dim in the small kitten brain:

A mouse tail flickering past,
Just beyond reach of his claws
Perhaps, or a ball of yarn
To be rolled to and fro on the floor.

Such force as he is supplied with
Must be exerted, it seems,
And what beyond this is the ultimate,
The divine purpose of cats?
—W. W. E. ROSS

THE CAT BALLET

Waiting centuries for his mistress,
the German Shepherd hunches on the lawn,
blinking in meditation
beside dishes of food and water.
Not alone. The new kitten —
more red than white —
waits too, in her fashion.

"That breathing rock, I'll climb it."
Digging her needles into skin,
Tumbles down with a feline laugh.

Runs to the fenced flowers;
With a jump like wings
returns in a challenging scratch.

Kitten in air after a dandelion puff
hears the growl for a stranger
(dog or man) at the gate.
Streaks to the barking rock . . .
curls up in his paws
like a mandarin orange.
— EVE TRIEM

CATS ON THE PROWL

CAT ON THE PORCH AT DUSK

Near the edge, as on a shelf,
The patient cat combines himself.
Motionless he huddles there
Before the changing light, and broods
On daylight's deep ineptitudes.

When gradually night takes its place,
He rises, stretching whiskers, toes,
And stepping royally, he goes.
Slowly the darkness slides apart
And soundless, lets him in.

— DOROTHY HARRIMAN

from THE CAT AND THE MOON

The cat went here and there
And the moon spun round like a top,
And the nearest kin of the moon,
The creeping cat, looked up.
Black Minnaloushe stared at the moon,
For, wander and wail as he would,
The pure cold light in the sky
Troubled his animal blood.

Minnaloushe runs in the grass
Lifting his delicate feet.
Do you dance, Minnaloushe, do you dance?
When two close kindred meet,
What better than call a dance:

Maybe the moon may learn,
Tired of that courtly fashion,
A new dance turn.
— WILLIAM BUTLER YEATS

A Garden Lion

O Michael, you are at once the enemy
And the chief ornament of our garden—
Scrambling up rose-posts, nibbling at nepeta,
Making your lair where tender plants should flourish,
Or proudly couchant on a sun-warmed stone.

What do you do all night there,
When we seek our soft beds,
And you go off, old roisterer,
Away into the dark?

I think you play at leopards and panthers;
I think you wander on to foreign properties;
But on winter mornings you are a lost orphan
Pitifully wailing underneath our windows.

And in summer, by the open doorway,
You come in *pad, pad,* lazily to breakfast,
Plumy tail waving, with a fine swagger,
Like a drum major, or a parish beadle,
Or a rich rajah, or a grand Mogul.
— EVELYN HAYES

SHE SIGHTS A BIRD

She sights a Bird—she chuckles—
She flattens—then she crawls—
She runs without the look of feet—
Her eyes increase to Balls.

Her Jaws stir—twitching—hungry—
Her Teeth can hardly stand—
She leaps, but Robin leaped the first—
Ah, Pussy, of the Sand.

The Hopes so juicy ripening—
You almost bathed your Tongue—
When Bliss disclosed a hundred Toes—
And fled with every one.
—EMILY DICKINSON

THE BIRD FANCIER

Up to his shoulders
In grasses coarse as silk,
The white cat with the yellow eyes
Sits with his paws together,
Tall as a quart of milk.
He hardly moves his head
To touch with neat nose
What his wary whiskers tell him
Is here a weed
And here a rose.
His sleepy eyes are wild with birds.
Every sparrow, thrush, and wren
Widens his eyes' furred horizons;
Then their flying song
Narrows them again.

    — JAMES KIRKUP

The Cat

The cat by magic zooms
Through slits of doors or air
To shadow through the rooms
And stalk what is not there.

And thrust outside by night,
With old and formal shout
In frightful guise she fights
The demons all about.

Then soft in sunny days,
Lulled in the leaves she goes.
No face of fiend dismays
Her vulnerable repose.

—ANN STANFORD

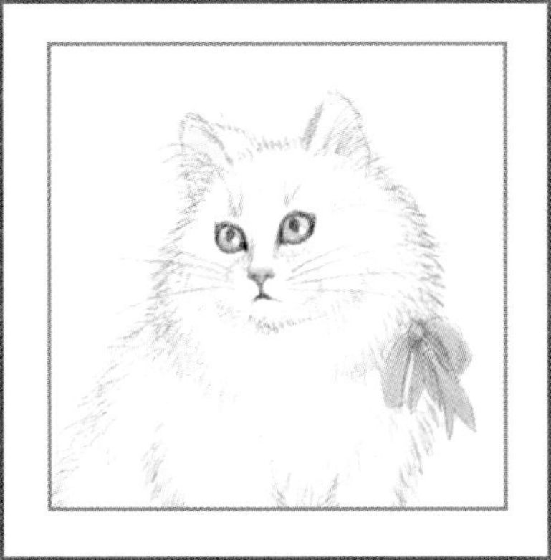

THE CAT WHOSE
NAME IS MOUSE

Has never seen one
but has become
a chaser of bees —
and been stung.
She is a moonlight,
midnight diva
in leaping and diving
ballets on the lawn,

star stalker of moths—
and she daggers them down.
Day's butterfly-leaper
captures mid-air.
Now summer's lean terror
sleeps plumply through winter.
I imagine her dreams
are a matter of wings.

—JOANNE DE LONGCHAMPS

INDOOR JUNGLE BLUES

Across the deep-piled jungle of our rooms,
he prowls the Persian patterns like a veldt
and winds his way among the window blooms
weaving the leaves and light with banded pelt.

In the striped daylight of venetian blinds
he stalks a memory of antelope
and wildebeest but almost never finds
a mouse to nourish atavistic hope.

Alert and cunning without need to be,
he flicks his tail, crouched on the ottoman,

ears crisped to sounds that shake tranquility—
the pouring milk, the shearing of a can.

He prowls the tropic warmth from door to door
and stares through his transparent walls of glass
at sudden gusts of birds that dart and soar
and scatter onto the fountain and the grass.

Across the indoor landscape of his days
he seeks escape from cage of pampered self,
dreams wildness, closing eyes of chrysoprase,
stretched on his high dark bough—the kitchen shelf.
—ULRICH TROUBETZKOY

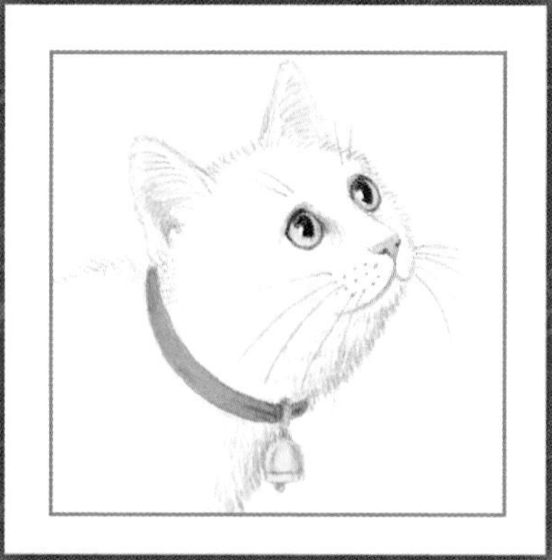

CAT IN MOONLIGHT

Through moonlight's milk
She slowly passes
As soft as silk
Between tall grasses.
I watch her go
So sleek and white—
As white as snow,
The moon so bright
I hardly know
White moon, white fur,
Which is the light
And which is her.

—DOUGLAS GIBSON

Cat

The fat cat on the mat
may seem to dream
of nice mice that suffice
for him, or cream;
but he free,
maybe,
walks in thought
unbowed, proud, where loud
roared and fought
his kin, lean and slim,
or deep in den
in the East feasted on beasts
and tender men.

POEMS FOR CAT LOVERS

The giant lion with iron
claw in paw,
and huge ruthless tooth
in gory jaw;
the pard dark-starred,
fleet upon feet,
that oft soft from aloft
leaps on his meat
where woods loom in gloom—
far now they be,
fierce and free,
and tamed as he;
but fat cat on the mat
kept as a pet,
he does not forget.
—J. R. R. TOLKIEN

ON A NIGHT OF SNOW

Cat, if you go outdoors you must walk in the snow.
You will come back with little white shoes on your feet,
Little white slippers of snow that have heels of sleet.
Stay by the fire, my Cat. Lie still, do not go.

See how the flames are leaping and hissing low,
I will bring you a saucer of milk like a marguerite,
So white and so smooth, so spherical, and so sweet—
Stay with me, Cat. Outdoors the wild winds blow.

Outdoors the wild winds blow, Mistress, and dark is the night.
Strange voices cry in the trees, intoning strange lore,
And more than cats move, lit by our eyes' green light,
On silent feet where the meadow grasses hang hoar—

Mistress, there are portents abroad of magic and might,
And things that are yet to be done. Open the door!
—Elizabeth J. Coatsworth

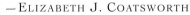

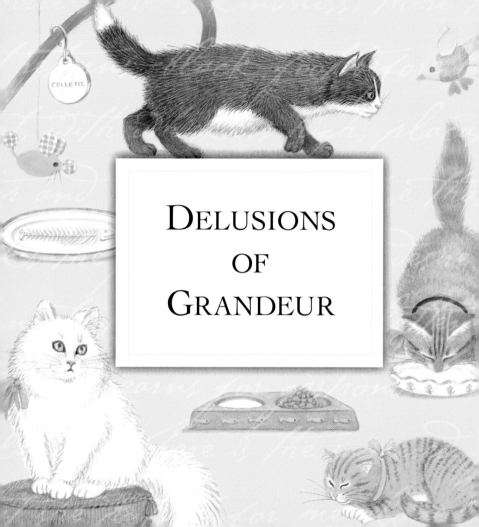

DELUSIONS
OF
GRANDEUR

A Modest Cat's Soliloquy

Far down within the damp dark earth
The grimy miner goes
That I on chilly nights may have
A fire to warm my toes.
Brave sailors plough the wintry main
Through peril and mishap,
That I, on Oriental rugs
May take my morning nap. . . .
The fish that swim the ocean
And the birds that fill the air —
Did I not like to pick their bones,
Pray, think you they'd be there?

— AUTHOR UNKNOWN

VAGABOND PRINCE

He came to us shadow-flat
But nevertheless a Cat
Spelled with a capital C,
And—we being what we were—
He's now the vast hauteur
Of ruffed rotundity.

A crisp, imperious mew,
When dinner, overdue,
Delays upon the shelf,

Reminds us of the need,
The privilege, indeed,
Of waiting on himself.

Both cream-fed pillow-sleeper
And gaunt-ribbed alley-creeper,
Who lacks an ear and eye—he
Could give a rajah lessons
How to confer his presence
On mere humanity.

—ANNE BARLOW

RETURN OF THE PRODIGAL

Where there is kindness, there the cat returns—
Black foot before black foot, with whiskers high,
Placating step, and hunger-lighted eye
That seeks the plate his whole desire burns
To fall upon. A flattened stomach yearns
For gastronomical felicity.
Where is the saucered milk that she
Puts by for me alone? Ulysses here returns!

If there are cats that, shadowed by the night,
Upon this sacred spot have placed their paws
And wolfed my fish, let them look to their claws!
There will be shrieks to make the darkness bright.
For braver men than I, love being gone,
Have trotted home for food with whiskers torn.

—FRANCES MINTURN HOWARD

CATALOG

Cats sleep fat and walk thin.
Cats, when they sleep, slump;
When they wake, pull in —
And where the plump's been
There's skin.
Cats walk thin.

Cats wait in a lump,
Jump in a streak.
Cats, when they jump, are sleek
As a grape slipping its skin —
They have technique.
Oh, cats don't creak.
They sneak.

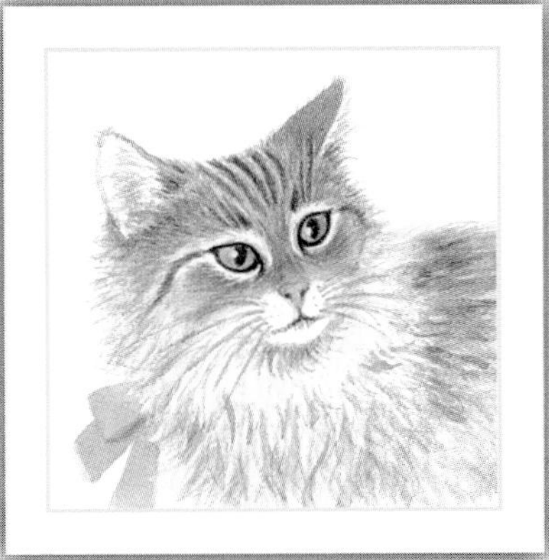

Cats sleep fat.
They spread comfort beneath them
Like a good mat,
As if they picked the place
And then sat.
You walk around one
As if he were the City Hall
After that.

If male,
A cat is apt to sing upon a major scale:
This concert is for everybody, this
Is wholesale.
For a baton, he wields a tail.

POEMS FOR CAT LOVERS

(He is also found,
When happy, to resound
With an enclosed and private sound.)

A cat condenses.
He pulls in his tail to go under bridges,
And himself to go under fences.
Cats fit
In any size box or kit;
And if a large pumpkin grew under one,
He could arch over it.

When everyone else is just ready to go out,
The cat is just ready to come in.
He's not where he's been.
Cats sleep fat and walk thin.

— ROSALIE MOORE

A CAT'S CONSCIENCE

A dog will often steal a bone;
But conscience lets him not alone,
And by his tail his guilt is known.

But cats consider theft a game,
And, howsoever you may blame,
Refuse the slightest sign of shame.

When food mysteriously goes,
The chances are that Pussy knows
More than she leads you to suppose.

And hence there is no need for you,
If Puss declines a meal or two,
To feel her pulse and make ado.
—AUTHOR UNKNOWN

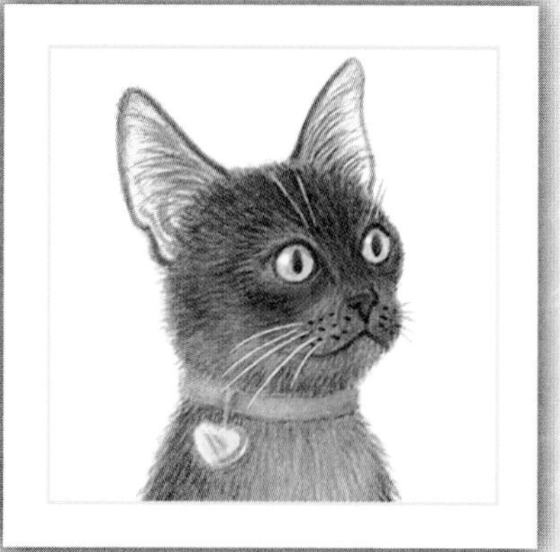

Radar Screen

The scoop of the cat's ear
catches sounds small enough
to go through a sieve, a screen,
a fine mesh. The scoop
swerves toward a noise, capturing it
with a flick either to keep it
in a little bin of knowledge or
to toss it out with another flick,
ready to scoop again any time.

—JEAN HARPER

THE CAT NAMED COLLETTE

She was spidery, a flower-small kitten—
creature of angles and tangents.
Whims formed her decisions.
She danced on a web of her making,
conjuring, conquering victims.
Like spiked leaf or pointed blossom,
she lived midair.

She is now, curved petal on petal,
an enormous peony:
the actress pleased with herself,
perfecting rites of indolence,
performing the role of her roundness.
She wears, always, white furs
whose dense folds are golden.

She keeps the delicate chin of her namesake,
the thin Sphinx smile.
Her intense, theatrical gaze,
beaming from black-ringed eyes,
is rich with self-love.

—JOANNE DE LONGCHAMPS

DELUSIONS OF GRANDEUR

CATS

Cats sleep
Anywhere,
Any table,
Any chair,
Top of piano,
Window-ledge,
In the middle,
On the edge,
Open drawer,
Empty shoe,

POEMS FOR CAT LOVERS

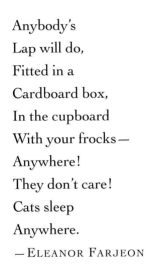

Anybody's
Lap will do,
Fitted in a
Cardboard box,
In the cupboard
With your frocks—
Anywhere!
They don't care!
Cats sleep
Anywhere.
—ELEANOR FARJEON

PROCESSION

Stiller than zeros of silence, Cat comes in
with minus quantities of quiet, spun
in a nought of attic on some nulling loom.
His yardages of hush in our loud room
he's wearing: sovereign cape from tongue to tail.
Pervasive plush, it nudges us and we kneel
to lift the hem from rubbing our clumsy shoe.
We clear the royal passage. The least we can do.
— NORMA FARBER

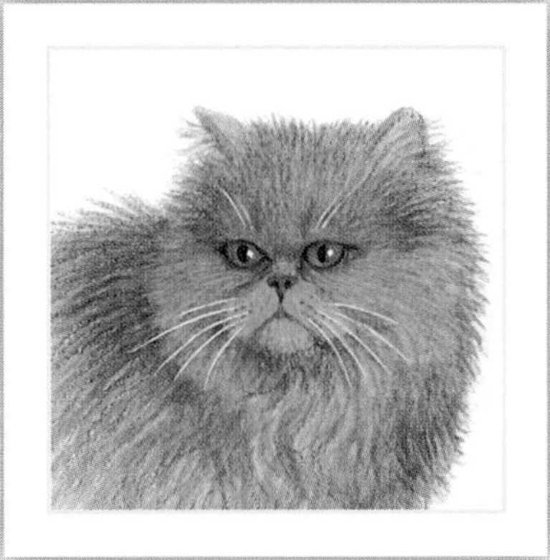

The Open Door

Out of the dark
to the sill of the door
lay the snow in a long,
unruffled floor;
and the lamplight fell
narrow and thin,
a carpet unrolled
for the cat to walk in.
Slowly, smoothly,
black as the night,
with paws unseen
(white upon white)
like a queen who walks
down a corridor,
the black cat paced

that cold, smooth floor—
and left behind her,
bead upon bead,
the track of small feet
little dark fern seed.

—ELIZABETH COATSWORTH

DELUSIONS OF GRANDEUR   63

MY FELINE
FAMILIAR

PORTRAIT OF A YOUNG CAT

If you would know my cat:
  he moves like the wind in the reeds;
black as spilled ink and paper-white are his furs;
when he shakes his head,
  his eyes make a bright half-circle of beads.
At a touch, he explodes
  like a snapdragon into loud purrs.
—ELIZABETH J. COATSWORTH

If Black

I have a cat, and if black is apropos,
an eternal no—
except for his round gold eyes that greenishly glow
and the fleet way he plays,
leaping to toss whatever it is with his paws,

while those needles of white flick at the ends of his toes.
He's a quickness that flows
more than it runs, a dainty panther of poise
as he noiselessly goes
night black from the tip of his tail to his nose.

In some ways a symbolic cat, but unlike those
snarling, obscene
black cats arched for evil's Halloween
or told of by Poe,
he's not so much metaphor dark as a lightfooted show—

a living example of just how wrong we can be
when we think we see
bad luck when we don't, and that we lack
perception, in fact,
when we call a cat something else because it is black.

—HAROLD WITT

MY FELINE FAMILIAR

TIGGER

Tigger rubs his whiskers against my whiskers
to thank me for the dust he rolls in,
and kneads my knees with tree-sharpened claws
to tell me he is the boss.
He spots buttercup butterflies in the autumn leaves
and pretends to keep secrets
from the last of the summertime bees.
He thinks he hides in the cedar bushes
then flops over in the greenest grass he can find
and makes the afternoon a poem.

—H. McAden Burwell

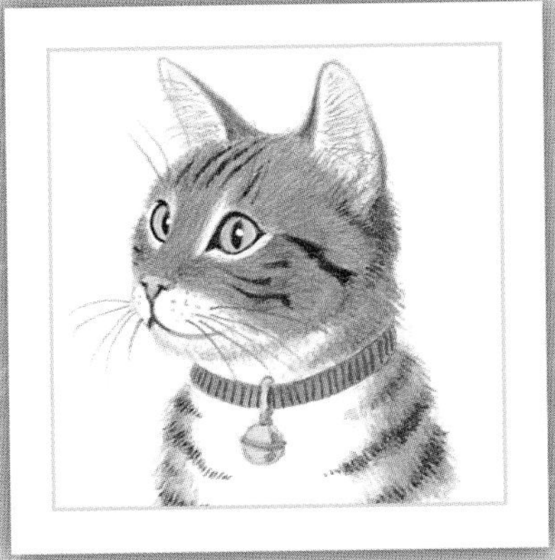

In Honor of Taffy Topaz

Taffy, the topaz-colored cat,
Thinks now of this and now of that,
But chiefly of his meals.
Asparagus, and cream, and fish
Are objects of his Freudian wish;
What you don't give, he steals.

His gallant heart is strongly stirred
By chink of plate or flight of bird;
He has a plumy tail;
At night he treads of stealthy pad
As merry as Sir Galahad
A-seeking of the Grail.

His amiable amber eyes
Are very friendly, very wise;
Like Buddha, grave and fat,
He sits, regardless of applause,
And thinking, as he kneads his paws,
What fun to be a cat!
—CHRISTOPHER MORLEY

MY FELINE FAMILIAR

TO PUFFIN, A WHITE CAT

On the dark blue rug that is a midnight sky,
The creamy saucer fills its heaven like a moon.
And over it a cat's white face
Basks in muted ecstasy,
Lapping the milky way to paradise
With near-shut golden eyes, pearled beard,
  and rosy mouth —
A cosy mask, lit by contentment from within
And by reflected radiance from beneath,
Where, like true benevolence, eclipsing its
  material cause,

The saucer, empty, still illuminates,
While Puffin sits and contemplates
Infinity's great O, the starry silk
Of dreams that only can be patched with milk.

Until the want is satisfied, for joy he softly roars,
And kneads his milky firmament with omnipresent paws.

—JAMES KIRKUP

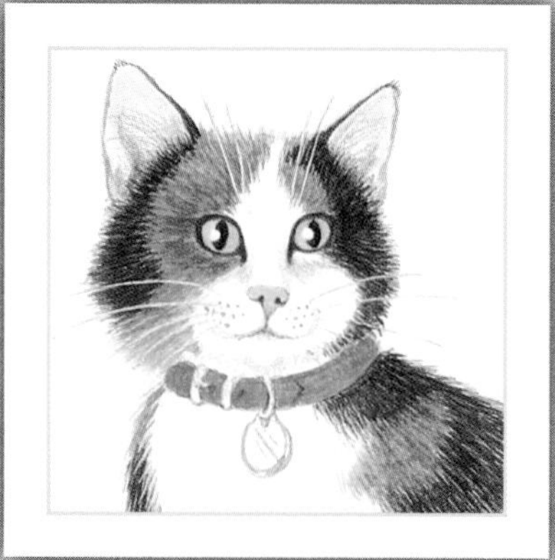

This Cat

This cat
Walks into the room and across the floor,
Under a chair, around the bed,
Behind the table and out the door.
I'm sitting on the chair
And I don't see where he is.
I don't see one hair of his.
I just hear the floorboards scarcely squeak.
This cat comes and goes
On invisible toes.
The sneak.

— KARLA KUSKIN

POLKA DOT

Is more than cat,
inviolate feline personality
with progeny for proof,
white and tawny,
a kind of calico cat
darkened to a trace of sherry
in an afternoon glass;
quietly dusting her nose
in red petunias
she looks to the window;
if I call "hey cat"
walks with ginger steps
to sit beside her outside dish
where sun dials away the summer

like dill in season,
eyes soft as early amber
shine and cover daylight.

Waiting for tuna,
waiting for her kittens
that from the roundness of her
could arrive at any minute,
she licks mittened paws,
sniffs a broken rose,
leaps to a monarch butterfly
strayed from a lost migration,
and finally gazes with longing
at cardinals in the tree
she will not climb.

— DAVID LOCHER

MY FELINE FAMILIAR

CINNAMON THE CAT

His a more mysterious spice
than common condiment,
his giving is not sharp
or quickened with the easy, trite
flow of salt and pepper's black and white,
for he is golden.

He faces you a bit apart,
contemplative.
He meditates.
His eyes are more than sad
as if beneath all feeling
were all knowing.

To end an interview
he turns his back and sits
motionless,
a Buddha
except his ears that twitch to catch
what comes or goes behind him.

For those of quiet taste
he has a subtle flavor,
unforgettable.
—HORTENSE ROBERTA ROBERTS

FOR A YELLOW CAT
AT MIDNIGHT

As though drifted inland
in some dark current of your own,
you settle against my side,
cumbrous as clay or a warm stone,
and I wake to find you there.

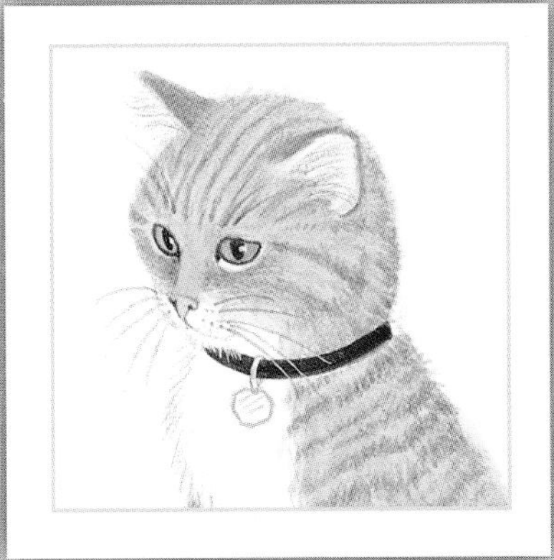

Why at night, small lion,
are you so much heavier than by day?
Only this afternoon
you slept, upside down, in a lap
already full of books and child,
and you were a tawny feather,
a fluff of sun.

POEMS FOR CAT LOVERS

Now pulled hard to the earth's center,
as though to a final place,
(lion, are we older by a night?)
we wait for sleep,
held fast by separate stars,
ponderous with what we do not know,
caught in a common dark.

—JEAN BURDEN

TITLE INDEX

Author Index

FIRST LINE INDEX

ACKNOWLEDGMENTS *(continued from p. 4)*

Copyright © 1975 and 1980 by Karla Kuskin. Reprinted by permission of Scott Treimel, NY. MOORE, ROSALIE. "Catalog." Originally printed in *The New Yorker*. Copyright © 1940 and renewed 1968. Reprinted by permission. SERRAILLIER, IAN. "Miss Tibbles" from *The Monster Horse*. Copyright © 1950 by Ian Serraillier. Published by Oxford University Press. Used by permission of Anne Serraillier. TOLKIEN, J.R.R. "CAT" from *The Adventures of Tom Bombadil* by J.R.R. Tolkien. Copyright © 1962 by Unwin Hyman Ltd. Copyright © renewed 1990 by Christopher R. Tolkien and Priscilla M.A.R. Tolkien. Reprinted by permission of Houghton Mifflin Company. WORTH, VALERIE. "Kitten" from *All the Small Poems and Fourteen More* by Valerie Worth. Copyright © 1987, 1994 by Valerie Worth. Reprinted by permission of Farrar, Straus and Giroux, LLC. YOLEN, JANE. "Mother Cat's Purr" from *Dragon Night and Other Lullabies*. Copyright © 1981 by Jane Yolen. Published by Methuen. Used by permission of Curtis Brown, Ltd.

While every effort has been made to establish ownership and use of each selection in this book, this has not always been possible. If contacted, the publisher will be pleased to rectify any inadvertent errors or omissions in subsequent editions.

d, as if beneath all feeling

urns his back and sits motion

catch what comes or goes ber

btle flavor unforgettable.

editates. His eyes are more tha

nowing. To end an interview

cept his ears that twitch to c

quiet taste, he has a subtle